NATIONAL GEOGRAPHIC KiDS

A FACT FOR EVERY DAY OF THE YEAR

365
FACTS TO MAKE YOU SAY...
WOW!

Published by Collins
An imprint of HarperCollins Publishers
Westerhill Road
Bishopbriggs
Glasgow G64 2QT
www.harpercollins.co.uk

HarperCollins Publishers
Macken House, 39/40 Mayor Street Upper, Dublin 1,
D01 C9W8, Ireland

In association with National Geographic Partners, LLC

NATIONAL GEOGRAPHIC and the Yellow Border Design are
trademarks of the National Geographic Society, used
under license.

First published 2022

ISBN 978-0-00-853298-7

10 9 8 7

If you would like to comment on any aspect of this book,
please contact us at the above address or online.
natgeokidsbooks.co.uk
collins.reference@harpercollins.co.uk

Acknowledgements
Publisher: Michelle I'Anson
Head of Creative Services: Craig Balfour
Text: Richard Happer
Typesetter: QBS
Editorial: Frances Cooper, Jill Laidlaw, Beth Ralston, Lauren
Reid and Evangeline Sellers
Cover design: Kevin Robbins

Images
P6 London Underground © Artokoloro/Alamy Stock Photo;
P12 Crown Jewels © Granger/Shutterstock; P37 Sky Brown
© Sipa US/Alamy Stock Photo; P53 Walt Disney © Glasshouse
Images/Shutterstock; P110 City Montessori School ©
Dheeraj Dhawan/Hindustan Times/Shutterstock; P115
Jacques Cousteau © Everett/Shutterstock; P119 Dolly the
Sheep © M Y Agency/Shutterstock

All other images © Shutterstock.

A FACT FOR EVERY DAY OF THE YEAR

365 FACTS TO MAKE YOU SAY... WOW!

1 JANUARY

WOOLLY MAMMOTHS roamed the Earth while the pyramids were being built. The last mammoths died out in 1650 BCE on Russia's Wrangel Island. The Great Pyramid of Giza was already 1,000 years old at this time!

Brilliant beast!

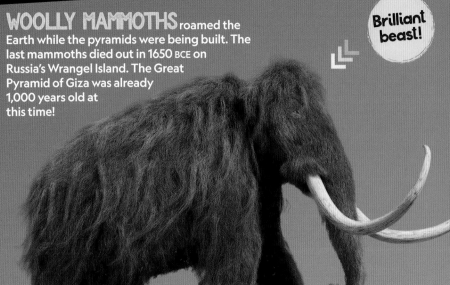

2 JANUARY

LOCH NESS in Scotland has more fresh water than all the rivers and lakes in England and Wales combined. There also may be more monsters!

3 JANUARY

BUTTERFLIES taste through their feet! Their feet have taste sensors that act like human taste buds. When they land on plants, they use these sensors to see if the plant is edible.

4 JANUARY

HONEY never goes bad. Archaeologists have found jars of honey in Egyptian tombs that are 3,000 years old – they tried it and it tasted delicious!

5 JANUARY

OCTOPUSES have 3 HEARTS.
They also have 9 BRAINS – a 'MAIN BRAIN'
and a 'MINI BRAIN' in each of their 8 ARMS.

6 JANUARY

Out of this world!

MERCURY is the planet nearest to the Sun. Did you know that craters on Mercury are named after famous musicians and writers? There is a 'Walt Disney crater' and a 'Tolkien crater', named after the author of *The Hobbit*.

7 JANUARY

If you could fold a piece of PAPER in half 42 times it would be thick enough to reach the moon.

8 JANUARY

CAN OPENERS were invented 48 years after cans. Before then you had to open your can of food with a hammer and chisel.

9 JANUARY

Super science

ELEMENTS are pure substances that combine to make up all matter. There are 118 elements, but not all of them can be found in nature. Some were even created in laboratories.

On this day...

10 JANUARY

THE LONDON UNDERGROUND opened on this day in 1863. Nicknamed 'the Tube', it is the world's oldest underground passenger railway. Today the Tube has 272 stations, 402 kilometres of track and is used by around 2 million people every day.

11 JANUARY

VATICAN CITY

is the smallest country in the world. It covers just 0.49 km² and is completely surrounded by Rome. There are no borders or passport controls into the state, but it does have its own stamps.

12 JANUARY

COMETS are lumps of **DIRTY ICE** and **ROCK** that have an **OVAL ORBIT** around the **SUN**.

As they get closer to the Sun they **HEAT UP** and **JETS OF VAPOUR** shoot out into a **SPECTACULAR TAIL**. A comet's tail can be **100 MILLION KILOMETRES LONG**.

13 JANUARY

WILLIAM SHAKESPEARE'S

plays have been performed more than any other writer's. When he wrote his plays, women were not allowed to act on stage so the female parts were played by men. Audiences were sometimes very rowdy and would shout, boo and throw food at any actors they didn't like!

14 JANUARY

GANGKHAR PUENSUM

in Bhutan is the tallest mountain that has not been climbed yet. It stands 7,570 metres tall. Climbers are banned because the mountain is so important to local religions.

15 JANUARY

Awesome animal

CLOWNFISH

keep safe by COVERING THEIR BODY in THICK MUCUS. This lets them HIDE amongst the stinging TENTACLES of SEA ANEMONES. where PREDATORS dare not go.

5 JANUARY

Every **STAR** that you can see with the naked eye is in our own galaxy, the Milky Way. The Milky Way has over 100 billion stars. There are between 100 and 200 billion other galaxies in the universe. So, there are approximately 10 billion trillion stars in the universe. That is more stars than there are grains of sand on all the beaches on Earth.

17 JANUARY

An **ICE AGE** is when the Earth's temperature drops by a lot for a long time. Glaciers and icefields at the poles can grow to cover land and sea that is normally warm. During the last ice age 11,700 years ago, northern Europe was covered by sheets of ice several kilometres thick.

Cool clouds

18 JANUARY

A **CUMULUS CLOUD** weighs 500 tonnes. These fluffy clouds might look like puffs of airy nothing, but they actually hold large amounts of water vapour.

19 JANUARY

You get more PIZZA from one 18-inch pizza than from two 12-inch pizzas! A single 18-inch pizza measures 254.47 square inches. Two 12-inch pizzas only total 226.2 square inches. And although it has a greater area, the 18-inch pizza has less crust than the two 12-inch pizzas!

20 JANUARY

The ARAL SEA was once the world's fourth-largest lake. But the water that flowed into it was diverted to irrigate fields and the Aral Sea began to shrink. The lake had an area of 68,000 km² in 1960 but it is now just 10% of its former size. The loss of the Aral Sea is one of the world's worst environmental disasters.

21 JANUARY

The world's largest manufacturer of TYRES is LEGO! They make approximately 700 MILLION tiny toy tyres every year – that's FAR MORE than any manufacturer of tyres for 'GROWN UP' cars or buses.

22 JANUARY

The **IGUAZU FALLS** are made of 275 separate waterfalls and stretch for 2.7 kilometres. The falls straddle the border between Argentina and Brazil. The jungles around the falls are home to jaguars, monkeys and toucans.

23 JANUARY

OXYGEN is the most common element in the Earth's crust, making up 46.6% of the crust by weight. It occurs in combination with other elements in substances called oxides. Silicon is the next most abundant element, making up 27.7% of the crust.

24 JANUARY

JAI ALAI is the fastest ball sport in the world. Expert players can sling the ball, known as a pelota, at over 300 km/h. The pelota is a little smaller than a cricket ball and harder than a golf ball and players use a curved basket to sling it.

25 JANUARY

ROBERT BURNS, a famous Scottish poet, was born on this day. 'Burns Suppers' are held every year on this date to celebrate his life and works. There are over 60 statues of Robert Burns around the world, more than any other non-religious person, after Queen Victoria and Christopher Columbus.

On this day...

26 JANUARY

The **CULLINAN DIAMOND** – the LARGEST DIAMOND in the WORLD – was discovered on this day in 1905. The ROUGH STONE was cut into **105** smaller stones. The biggest of these is still the largest diamond in the world and is part of the **ENGLISH CROWN JEWELS.**

On this day...

27 JANUARY

GEYSERS are volcanic springs that shoot hot water and steam into the air. Steamboat Geyser in Yellowstone National Park, USA, is the world's tallest geyser and can erupt to a height of over 91 metres. Yellowstone has over 500 geysers – half of all the geysers in the world.

28 JANUARY

NICOBAR PIGEONS are the closest living relative to the extinct dodo. These rare birds can be found in the Andaman Islands of India and in New Guinea. They have vibrant plumage, with blue, green and copper tones as well as a white tail.

29 JANUARY

SNAILS

have more teeth than any other animal on the planet. A garden snail has around 14,000 teeth! One type of sea snail –the limpet –has teeth that are made from the strongest biological material on Earth.

30 JANUARY

A person with the jumping skills of a **FLEA** would be able to leap over St Paul's Cathedral! This tiny wingless insect can leap 200 times the length of its own body.

31 JANUARY

YELLOWSTONE NATIONAL PARK in the USA was the world's first national park. It was founded in 1872 with the aim of protecting the area's unique landscape, plant and animal life. Today there are 6,555 national parks around the world.

13

1 FEBRUARY

QUETZALCOATLUS

was a pterosaur that was as tall as a giraffe. It stood 5–6 metres tall with a wingspan of up to 11 metres. It was the largest flying animal that ever lived.

2 FEBRUARY

The Caribbean island of TRINIDAD has the world's largest lake – of tar! The Pitch Lake consists of black pitch, a type of tar-like crude oil. The lake is 60 metres deep. The explorer Sir Walter Raleigh visited the lake in 1595 and used its tar to seal the timbers of his ship.

3 FEBRUARY

TARANTULA

spiders are a tasty treat in Cambodia. The spiders are usually eaten fried. You can buy them by the handful from street carts. They are often rolled in garlic or sugar to give the taste some added bite.

4 FEBRUARY

SOUTHEND PIER in England is so long that it has its own railway line. The pier runs for over 2 kilometres out from Southend into the Thames Estuary. It is the longest pleasure pier in the world.

Groovy gaming

5 FEBRUARY

The **PLAYSTATION 2** is the most **POPULAR** video games console of all time. It launched in 2000 and has sold more than **155 MILLION CONSOLES**, which is more than the XBox 360 and the Nintendo Switch combined.

6 FEBRUARY

VENUS is the second planet from the Sun. Clouds of sulphuric acid swirl in its atmosphere. A day on Venus lasts for 243 Earth days – that's longer than the planet's year, which lasts 225 Earth days.

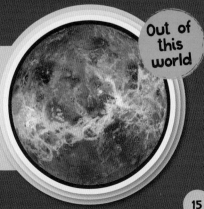

Out of this world

15

7 FEBRUARY

POLAR BEARS

have BLACK SKIN. Their fur REFLECTS white light, making the bears seem white. They are the LARGEST LAND CARNIVORE: an adult male polar bear is about 1.5 times taller than a male human and more than 5 times heavier. They can SWIM FOR DAYS at a time and spend half their lives looking for their next meal.

8 FEBRUARY

The AMAZON is the world's largest river. It flows for 6,992 kilometres, making it nearly as long as the Nile. But the Amazon contains much, much more water. The Amazon has more water than the next 7 largest rivers combined. There are no bridges over the Amazon.

9 FEBRUARY

MICHAEL PHELPS is an American swimmer that has won more Olympic medals than any other athlete – a total of 28. The next best tally is 18 medals by gymnast Larisa Latynina. Phelps won the most medals at 4 Olympic Games in a row: Athens 2004, Beijing 2008, London 2012 and Rio 2016.

10 FEBRUARY

The SUN weighs 700 times more than all the other planets in our solar system combined. It would take 1.3 million Earths to fill the Sun's volume!

11 FEBRUARY

Even if a PIG could fly, other pigs wouldn't be able to see it, as they're incapable of looking up! The anatomy of their neck muscles and spine limits the movement of their head, so they can't look directly upwards.

12 FEBRUARY

There are 195 COUNTRIES in the world. In 2013, Graham Hughes from Liverpool set a record for the fastest time to visit all countries without flying, which took him 4 years and 31 days!

13 FEBRUARY

A METEOROID is a lump of space rock. If it burns up while entering Earth's atmosphere it's called a meteor. If a piece lands, then it's called a meteorite. The largest meteorite found is the Hoba Meteorite. It weighs 60 tonnes and is still sitting in Namibia, Africa, where it smashed down 80,000 years ago.

14 FEBRUARY

The search engine GOOGLE is named after the number 'googol', which is 1 followed by 100 zeroes. If the whole universe was packed with sand there would still be fewer than a googol grains.

15 FEBRUARY

You cannot start an AVALANCHE by shouting. This might happen in the movies, but in reality your voice doesn't create enough force to make snow slide off a mountain. However, walking in the wrong spot can cause an avalanche if the conditions are right, and so too can a strong wind!

16 FEBRUARY

On this day...

On this day in 1923 the tomb of Egyptian King TUTANKHAMUN was opened 3,250 years after it had been sealed. Archaeologist Howard Carter feasted his eyes on ancient royal riches including golden masks, weapons, thrones, trumpets, food and wine, and a solid gold coffin.

17 FEBRUARY

Fabulous fruit

A juicy PINEAPPLE takes 2 or even 3 years to grow. Each plant produces only one fruit at a time. Pineapples were a status symbol in 18th-century England – they were so cool that you could rent one to take to a party!

18 FEBRUARY

The tiny **TARDIGRADE** might well be the TOUGHEST CREATURE ON EARTH. Also known as the 'WATER BEAR', this 1-millimetre-long animal is nearly INDESTRUCTIBLE. They can withstand temperatures as low as −200°C as well as RADIATION, BOILING LIQUIDS, and up to 6 times the pressure of the deepest part of the ocean. They can even survive in the VACUUM OF SPACE!

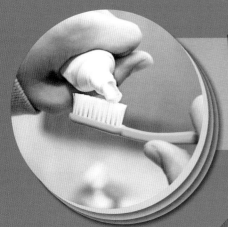

19 FEBRUARY

The little blob of TOOTHPASTE on your brush is called a nurdle. The dot on top of i and j is called a tittle. The tag on the end of your shoelaces is called an aglet.

20 FEBRUARY

Switzerland's mountain slopes are a SKIING paradise. But the SNOWSPORT wasn't known in the country until 1893 when it was popularised there by SIR ARTHUR CONAN DOYLE – the creator of the famous detective SHERLOCK HOLMES!

21 FEBRUARY

There is a scientific measure for how blue the ocean is! Next time you see the sea, take a picture and you can grade it on the FOREL-ULE SCALE: the scale for measuring the blueness of bodies of water!

22 FEBRUARY

Humans have been JUGGLING for at least 4,000 years! There are paintings of juggling girls on the walls of Ancient Egyptian tombs. In 2012 16-year-old Alex Barron became the first person ever to juggle 11 balls.

23 FEBRUARY

EARTH is tilted on its axis at an angle of 23°. The angle at which the Sun's rays strike the planet changes from month to month. This is what causes the seasons.

What on Earth?

24 FEBRUARY

Countries in mid to high LATITUDES get the greatest variation in heat and light over the year and usually have 4 seasons. In the Tropics, the powerful Sun is overhead, and there are 2 seasons. At the Equator there is just 1 season.

25 FEBRUARY

ORANGUTANS get their name from the Malay words 'orang hutan' which translates to 'human of the forest'. This description is accurate because these red-haired apes share almost 97% of the same DNA as humans! Orangutans are native to Sumatra and Borneo in southeast Asia, where they can be found amongst the trees of the tropical rainforest.

26 FEBRUARY

ENGLISH is the most-spoken language in the world, with 1.132 billion speakers. Mandarin is the second-most spoken language with 1.117 billion speakers.

27 FEBRUARY

A **MONSOON** is a wind that blows at a certain time of year and lasts for a whole season. The monsoon in India brings huge amounts of rain in June and July. It can cause dangerous floods but it is also vital for crops.

Wild weather

28 FEBRUARY

An **AQUEDUCT** is a bridge that carries water. The Romans were master aqueduct builders and built them throughout their empire. Rome had 770 kilometres of aqueducts which carried over a billion litres of fresh water every day. The Pont du Gard aqueduct in France has 3 levels and is 48.8 metres high.

29 FEBRUARY

The Earth takes 365 days and 6 hours to orbit the Sun. After 4 years, these extra 6 hours have made the seasons a whole day behind the calendar. So, we add an **EXTRA DAY** – today, 29 February – to correct this.

1 MARCH

The SHANGHAI MAGLEV train doesn't have wheels. MAGNETS lift the train above the track and make it move – and it moves REALLY FAST! This MAGLEV is one of the FASTEST TRAINS in the world with a top speed of over 430 KM/H.

Terrific transport

2 MARCH

The NILE is the world's longest river. It flows for 6,650 kilometres through 11 countries to reach the Mediterranean Sea. The Nile has been important to human civilisation for thousands of years, providing water for crops and a means of transport.

3 MARCH

OLYMPIC GOLD MEDALS are 92.5% silver. The outside of the medal is plated with gold. Olympic silver medals are real silver. Bronze medals are actually made of brass, a mixture of 95% copper and 5% zinc.

4 MARCH

The **INTERNATIONAL SPACE STATION** orbits the Earth once every 90 minutes. It is the second-brightest object in the night sky after the Moon and is easily visible with the naked eye. The space station orbits about 400 kilometres above the planet's surface. It was launched in 1998.

5 MARCH

On this day...

On this day in 2015 the town of **CAPRACOTTA** in Italy was blanketed with a record 2.56 metres of snow in just 24 hours.

6 MARCH

EARTH is 150 million kilometres from the Sun. Every year we travel on a 1 billion kilometre orbit around the Sun, travelling at 108,000 km/h.

7 MARCH

POMPEII is the world's largest archaeological site. The Roman city was covered with 25 metres of ash and lava when the volcano Vesuvius erupted in 79 CE. Pompeii was lost for 1500 years until it was accidentally rediscovered by Italian architect Domenico Fontana in 1599 while he was digging a water tunnel.

8 MARCH

VIKINGS didn't wear horned helmets. Horns were added to the Viking 'look' by creative artists in the 19th century. The only real Viking helmet found was a simple round shape with a small peak.

9 MARCH

URANIUM is the heaviest element that forms naturally. Uranium is radioactive, meaning it can give out energy as radiation. A uranium fuel pellet the size of your fingertip has the same energy as 800 kilograms of coal.

10 MARCH

ROGUE WAVES are waves that are much larger than the other waves around them and which seem to appear unexpectedly. They can reach up to 30 metres high. They are so big that satellites can detect them.

11 MARCH

NORTHERN LIGHTS can be seen thanks to the EARTH'S MAGNETIC FIELD. These spectacular, SHIMMERING LIGHTS appear in the NORTHERN NIGHT SKY and are also called the AURORA BOREALIS. Tiny particles streaming from the Sun, called the SOLAR WIND, hit Earth's magnetic field and cause the LIGHTSHOW.

Spectacular skies

27

12 MARCH

The **LILAC BREASTED ROLLER** is the **NATIONAL BIRD OF KENYA**. The bird's feathers are made up of various **COLOURS** – brown, green, white, yellow, black, turquoise, blue and lilac. These different colours are said to reflect the different **TRIBES** that make up the **COMMUNITY** of the country.

Brilliant bird!

13 MARCH

The greatest **TIDAL RANGE** (the height difference between high tide and low tide) in the world is in Bay of Fundy in Nova Scotia, Canada, where the difference can be up to 16.3 metres.

14 MARCH

The eyes of a cat shining at night led to a very useful invention. Percy Shaw from Yorkshire saw the puss's pupils gleaming in his car lights on the way home one evening in 1934. He later created reflecting road studs – now known as **CAT'S EYES**.

Fast flapper

15 MARCH

The buzzing that **BEES** make is the sound of their wings beating. Honey bees can beat their wings over 230 times every second.

16 MARCH

BIRMINGHAM has more kilometres of canal than Venice. The city was the hub of England's canal network and a vital trade centre. It has 56 kilometres of canals. Venice's streets are virtually all canal, but the city is small and in total there are only 42 kilometres of canal.

17 MARCH

When **APHID** babies are born they are already pregnant with their future children! These garden insects are like Russian dolls, with the next generation growing inside the baby that is growing inside its mother.

18 MARCH

The **SEAWISE GIANT** was the **LARGEST** and **HEAVIEST SHIP** ever built. This oil **SUPERTANKER** was 458 metres long, weighed 657,019 tonnes and was **TOO BIG** to navigate the **ENGLISH CHANNEL**, the **SUEZ CANAL** or the **PANAMA CANAL**. Sadly it was scrapped in 2010.

19 MARCH

A strawberry isn't a berry, but a **BANANA** is! To botanists, a true berry has 3 parts: an outside skin, a fleshy inside, and seeds in the middle. But a strawberry has its seeds on the outside and is called an 'accessory fruit'. Grapes, oranges, kiwi fruit, cucumber, pumpkins, peppers and watermelon are true berries!

20 MARCH

On th day.

The spring **EQUINOX** usually falls on this day each year. There are 12 hours of daylight and 12 hours of night everywhere on Earth. The word 'equinox' comes from the Latin for 'equal night'. There is an autumn equinox around 22 September.

22 MARCH

MOUNT RUSHMORE is famous for having four huge faces of US presidents carved into its cliffs. The sculptures of George Washington, Thomas Jefferson, Theodore Roosevelt and Abraham Lincoln are 60 metres tall and can be seen from 97 kilometres away.

21 MARCH

BOBSLEIGH is a winter sport where teams race sleds down an ice-covered track at speeds of up to 150 km/h. The sport originated in Switzerland in the late 19th-century and was first included in the Winter Olympics in 1924.

23 MARCH

The **GOLIATH BIRDEATER** is the world's largest spider. It can weigh 175 grams and have a body measuring 13 centimetres long. The spider eats frogs, rodents, lizards and snakes – as well as birds.

24 MARCH

The first **SNOWMOBILE** was built and tested by Joseph-Armand Bombardier when he was only 15 years old. He perfected his design as the 'Ski-Doo'. This was meant to be called the 'Ski-Dog', but a printing mistake spelled it as 'Ski-Doo' and the name stuck!

25 MARCH

Are you brave enough to walk over the **ZHANGJIAJIE GLASS BRIDGE?** It stretches 430 metres across a canyon in China, and is suspended 300 metres above the ground below, making it the longest and tallest glass-bottomed bridge in the world.

26 MARCH

When we breathe our lungs take oxygen from the air and add it to our blood. But air is only 21% oxygen – 78% is **NITROGEN**, which our bodies have no need for. Nitrogen is very useful in other ways though – it's used to fill crisp packets to keep crisps fresh!

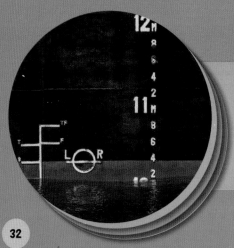

27 MARCH

A **PLIMSOLL LINE** is marked on the side of a ship to show how deep in the water it can safely sit when loaded with cargo. The line has different levels for seawater that is warmer and saltier. Plimsoll shoes are named after the line!

28 MARCH

A full **ORCHESTRA** has around 100 **MUSICIANS.** The orchestra grew from the smaller groups of musicians who played in **ROYAL COURTS** in the **17TH CENTURY.** The orchestra is led by the **CONDUCTOR,** who keeps time with a **BATON.**

Music makers

29 MARCH

The **IRON AGE** was a period of time that began around 1200 BCE. People in the eastern Mediterranean learned how to make tools, weapons, cooking pots, ploughs and nails. Iron was stronger than copper, the metal that people had used before. Using iron helped civilisation to develop rapidly.

30 MARCH

When **GLASS** breaks the cracks move through it at 4,800 km/h – that's over 5 times faster than a jet airliner, which travels up to 925 km/h.

31 MARCH

Exactly how long is a **METRE?** The standard measure used to be the length of a platinum bar kept in Paris. Today 1 metre is defined by scientists as being the precise distance that light travels in a vacuum in 1/299,792,458 of a second.

DOG FOOD is edible for humans too. Some people are employed as 'dog food tasters' to make sure that your four-legged friend's supper is as tasty as it can possibly be.

The **SALT** that you sprinkle on your food to make it tastier is made of a toxic metal and a poisonous gas! Salt is actually sodium chloride. Salt was so valuable in ancient Rome that soldiers were paid with it. The word 'salary' comes from the Latin word *sal*, for salt.

3 APRIL

BLUE WHALES are the **LARGEST ANIMALS** ever to have lived on **EARTH**. These **MARINE** mammals can grow to over **30 METRES** long and weigh more than **200 TONNES**. A blue whale's **TONGUE** alone can weigh as much as an **ELEPHANT** and its **HEART** can weigh as much as a **CAR**.

Colossal creature

34

4 APRIL

A **BLACK HOLE** is an area of space where gravity is so strong that nothing, not even light, can escape. Astronomers predicted black holes might exist before they were detected. Some black holes might have the mass of billions of suns.

5 APRIL

ARMADILLOS almost always give birth to identical quadruplets. The name 'armadillo' means 'little armoured one' in Spanish. Most armadillos roll into a ball when startled. Other species leap 1 metre straight up in the air.

Bird banter

6 APRIL

Ever heard a **BIRD TALK?** Many species including cockatoos, myna birds, parrots and crows can mimic human speech. One budgerigar, named Puck, broke the world record for the largest bird vocabulary – he knew more than 1,700 words!

7 APRIL

The **MOON** is 3,475 kilometres in diameter. That makes it almost as broad as Australia! The dark 'seas' on the Moon's surface are actually patches of lava.

8 APRIL

HYDROGEN makes up 75% of all matter in the Universe. It is the lightest element. When hydrogen burns it produces water. Its name means 'water-former'.

9 APRIL

The flag of NEPAL is the only national flag that isn't a rectangle or a square. It is formed of two triangular pennants joined together in a traditional shape. The flag is red to symbolise bravery and the colour of the rhododendron, Nepal's national flower. It has a blue border, which is the colour of peace.

10 APRIL

The PACIFIC OCEAN is the largest and deepest ocean on Earth. You could easily fit every country in the world inside it. It covers almost a third of the whole planet.

11 APRIL

When ICEBERG B-15 split off from Antarctica in March 2000 it was 295 kilometres long and 37 kilometres wide – that's larger than the island of Jamaica. This largest-ever iceberg floated around the Antarctic Ocean for 5 years before breaking into several pieces. One of these pieces, which measured 20 kilometres by 7 kilometres, was still travelling in 2021.

Super skater

12 APRIL

SKY BROWN is the **YOUNGEST** professional **SKATEBOARDER** in the world. At the age of 13, she competed for GREAT BRITAIN at the **2020 SUMMER OLYMPICS** in Tokyo, Japan, where she scooped a BRONZE MEDAL for the Park event.

13 APRIL

The world's largest **MIRROR** is actually a salt flat in Bolivia. The Salar de Uyuni is a super-flat salt flat, or playa, half the size of Wales. When rain falls the surface of the playa turns into a huge silver mirror.

14 APRIL

7% of all HUMANS who have ever lived are alive today. Around 108 billion people have ever existed in the history of the world, and 7.8 billion of them are on planet Earth right now.

15 APRIL

RMS TITANIC was the world's largest ship when it was launched. The ship was 269 metres long and could carry 3,320 people. Sadly it hit an iceberg on its maiden voyage and sank on this day in 1912. The wreck was found in 1985 lying 3,784 metres down in the cold north Atlantic.

On this day...

On this day...

16 APRIL

There is something very long and snake-like in the jungles of Malaysia – the world's largest waterslide! The ESCAPE SLIDE near Penang will whoosh you, twisting and turning, through the forest for 1,111 metres. Each run down the slide lasts for 3 minutes!

17 APRIL

On this day in 1938, modern SUPERHEROES were born! The first issue of *Action Comics* was published featuring Superman lifting a car above his head on the cover. Superman soon became one of the world's most popular characters.

18 APRIL

A teaspoon of a **NEUTRON STAR** would weigh more than **MOUNT EVEREST!** A neutron star is a collapsed star that is **INCREDIBLY DENSE.** A chunk of neutron star the size of a **WASHING MACHINE** would have the same mass as the entire **ATLANTIC OCEAN.**

19 APRIL

STARS twinkle when their light is bent by layers of air in Earth's atmosphere. The planets – including Jupiter, Saturn, Venus and Mars – do not usually twinkle, making them easy to recognise.

20 APRIL

The **INTERNATIONAL DATE LINE** is an imaginary line on the surface of Earth that runs from the North Pole to the South Pole. Just west of the line it is 12 hours ahead of Greenwich Mean Time (GMT) and just east of the line it is 12 hours behind. So when you cross the line you go either a whole day forwards or backwards in time.

Who knew?!

21 APRIL

YEAST is a vital ingredient in bread and it is actually a tiny living organism that is a type of fungus. The yeast eats sugar in the bread dough and excretes carbon dioxide – which makes the dough puff up into lovely bread!

22 APRIL

In a **FOOD CHAIN**, energy is passed from one species to another – a plant is eaten by an insect, this is eaten by a bird, the bird by a fox, the fox dies and decomposes into food for bacteria.

23 APRIL

The first **FIREWORKS** lit up the night skies of China over 1,000 years ago! They were brought to Europe by the 13th century and have been used to mark festivals and celebrations ever since.

24 APRIL

The **SAHARA DESERT** is the largest hot desert in the world and the third largest desert after Antarctica and the Arctic. If the Sahara was a country it would be the 5th largest in the world. It covers 9.2 million km² – almost the same area as China. The average annual temperature is 30°C and the hottest temperature ever recorded was 58°C.

Radical rabbits

25 APRIL

A single pair of **RABBITS** could create a **FAMILY** of **3.7 MILLION** rabbits in just 4 years. Rabbits can **BREED** when they are only 3 months old and can have a **LITTER** of babies every month.

LADYBIRDS come in many different COLOURS and PATTERNS. The most familar is the SEVEN-SPOT LADYBIRD with its red shell and black spots, however, there are other species that come in colours such as YELLOW, ORANGE and BLACK. These colours aren't just nice to look at. They act as a WARNING to PREDATORS.

Marvellous minibeast

27 APRIL

MECHANICAL CLOCKS
were invented in the early 14th century in Europe. A clock built in 1386 is still ticking today in Salisbury Cathedral in England. It has ticked more than 500 million times.

28 APRIL

TUNNEL BORING MACHINES
are giant machines that dig through the earth to create the holes for new train and road tunnels. They can tunnel under cities without disturbing the buildings above. They eat through dirt and rock at a rate of 18 metres a day!

29 APRIL

No two people see the exact same RAINBOW. A rainbow is formed when a source of light, usually sunlight, is bent and reflected in water droplets. So the rainbow you see always depends on your own position relative to the Sun. And no two people can be in the same place at the same time!

30 APRIL

The TROJAN HORSE is a famous trick from history. The ancient Greeks laid siege to the city of Troy. They left a wooden horse outside the city gates. The Trojans brought it inside, thinking it was a peace offering – but Greek soldiers were hiding inside the horse!

43

1 MAY

DOLPHINS often go 'surfing' in waves. They swim and leap through the crashing surf, and they do it simply for fun!

2 MAY

The **TAJ MAHAL** in India is one of the world's most famous landmarks. The white marble structure took 20,000 workers 22 years to build and was completed in 1653. The Taj Mahal is a famous symbol of love – the emperor Shah Jahan had it built as a memorial to his wife Mumtaz Mahal.

3 MAY

The **PLATYPUS** looks like a cross between a duck, an otter and a beaver. The first scientists to see platypuses thought someone was playing a prank on them! A platypus is a mammal that lays eggs. A baby platypus is called a puggle.

Sporting superstar

4 MAY

The **BALLON D'OR** (which is French for 'Golden Ball') and the Ballon d'Or Féminin are sports awards given every year to the best male and best female soccer players, respectively. The Ballon d'Or has been won a record eight times by Lionel Messi. Cristiano Ronaldo is close behind – he has won five times. The Ballon d'Or Féminin has been won by Ada Hegerberg, Megan Rapinoe, Alexia Putellas and Aitana Bonmatí.

5 MAY

MARATHONS are named after a battle. A soldier called Pheidippides ran 26 miles to Athens to announce the news of the Battle of Marathon in 490 BCE. He Shouted 'Nike!' (the Greek word for victory), then dropped dead from exhaustion.

6 MAY

The Romans named **MARS** after their god of war because the planet is a fiery red. This colour is from oxidised iron on the surface – Mars is literally rusting!

7 MAY

A human **VOICE** can shatter a glass. A drinks glass, like many objects, will vibrate at a certain frequency when forces act on it. If you can match that frequency with your voice – and hold it for several seconds – then the glass will shatter.

8 MAY

The deepest point in the oceans is the **CHALLENGER DEEP** in the Mariana Trench. It descends for 11,034 metres. You could drop Mount Everest in and it would be completely underwater.

9 MAY

All the world's continents were once joined together in a 'supercontinent' called **PANGEA.** This mega landmass began to break up 175 million years ago. But if you look at Africa and South America on a map you can see how they once fitted together!

10 MAY

Global **SEA LEVELS** are due to human-caused **GLOBAL WARMING**. Melting glaciers and **ICE SHEETS** cause more water to flow into the sea. From 1900 to 2017 the global sea level **ROSE** by 21 centimetres.

On this day...

12 MAY

The **INDUSTRIAL REVOLUTION** took place from 1760–1840 when new inventions changed people's lives and our landscapes forever. Steam power meant that factories could produce huge amounts of goods. Steam trains and ships whizzed people to new places and cities grew far beyond their old bounds. Britain's population increased by 60% in just 40 years.

11 MAY

On this day, the supercomputer **DEEP BLUE** became the first computer to win a chess match against a human champion in 1997. Deep Blue beat chess grandmaster Garry Kasparov 3½–2½ in the 6-game match.

13 MAY

MOZART was a musical prodigy – he was incredibly talented at a very young age. He began composing music when he was just 5 years old and played for royalty all over Europe from the age of 6. It is believed that Mozart wrote his first opera at the age of 12!

€ 0,80

14 MAY

Shuffle a deck of 52 **CARDS** and the sequence you get has almost certainly never occurred in the whole of human history. There are more ways to arrange a deck of cards than there are atoms on Earth – the number is 8 followed by 67 zeroes.

15 MAY

A **DELTA** is where a river meets the sea and deposits its sediment (solid material that is carried by the water). The delta of the Ganges river is the world's largest. It covers an area of 60,000 kilometres^2 – 3 times the size of Wales.

16 MAY

HINDUISM is a religion that is more than 3,000 years old. More than 900 million people practice Hinduism. Hindus worship many gods and believe in reincarnation – they believe that when someone dies their soul can return in human, animal, or even plant form.

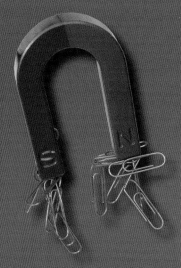

17 MAY

MAGNETS are made of materials that can create a magnetic field, such as the metals iron, nickel, cobalt, and steel. Magnets have a north pole and a south pole. The opposite poles of two magnets will attract each other, and the identical poles will push each other away.

18 MAY

The Earth's core is made of iron and nickel, and it generates a **MAGNETIC FIELD** around our planet. A compass needle aligns itself to this magnetic field, helping explorers find north. Birds also use the Earth's magnetic field to guide them home on their long-distance flights.

19 MAY

Every **SUNFLOWER** is a collection of thousands of tiny flowers. The yellow petals and fuzzy brown centre that make up a sunflower are individual flowers. There can be as many as 2,000 flowers on one sunflower.

Dapper dino

20 MAY

TYRANNOSAURUS REX LIVED NEARER to OUR TIME today than it did to fellow dinosaur **STEGOSAURUS**. T. Rex lived 66 MILLION YEARS AGO. Stegosaurus lived 155 million years ago – **89 MILLION YEARS EARLIER.**

49

On this
day...

21 MAY

FOSSILS are ancient organisms that got buried in sediment and then turned to rock over millions of years. Geologists can see which types of creatures lived, and when, by examining fossils trapped in layers of rock.

22 MAY

On this day in 2010, **JORDAN ROMERO** from California, USA, became the youngest person ever to climb Mount Everest. He was just 13 years old! Jordan had already climbed 5 of the highest peaks on the 7 continents before he made his historic climb.

23 MAY

CHARLES DARWIN was a naturalist who showed how animals could evolve into different species through the process of natural selection. He spent 5 years sailing the world on a ship called HMS *Beagle*, studying thousands of animals, plants and fossils, many of which had never been seen by people in Europe before.

24 MAY

ELECTRON MICROSCOPES uses a beam of tiny particles called electron to create a magnified picture of an object. Electron microscopes can magnify up to 10 million times, that is 5,000 times more powerful than the best optical microscope.

25 MAY

There are more than **7,100 LANGUAGES**
SPOKEN around the WORLD today. Approximately
200 LANGUAGES are spoken in EUROPE, while
more than 2,000 are spoken in ASIA.

Different LANGUAGES use DIFFERENT
ALPHABETS. The CAMBODIAN alphabet is the
LONGEST in the WORLD with 74 LETTERS!

26 MAY

The **SKY** is blue because the light that makes up sunlight is scattered by different amounts when it passes through the air in the atmosphere. Blue light has a shorter wavelength so it scatters more effectively. Redder light, with its longer wavelength, tends to pass on through the atmosphere with less scattering.

27 MAY

The **BRONZE AGE** is a period of time that began around 4,000 BCE. People in southeast Europe learned how to make tools from bronze, an alloy (mixture) of copper and tin. They travelled long distances to trade tin, which was only found in a few places. The oldest boats date from the Bronze Age.

28 MAY

OBSIDIAN is a type of volcanic glass that can form when molten rock cools very quickly. Stone age people used it to make arrowheads and it can be used to make blades 500 times sharper than the sharpest steel scalpel.

29 MAY

SKATEBOARDING was invented by surfers in California in the 1950s – they wanted something to do when there weren't any big waves to ride! The first boards were pieces of wooden boxes with the wheels from roller skates attached.

30 MAY

WALT DISNEY was a famous animator, founder of Disneyland and the original voice of Mickey Mouse. He won 22 'Oscars' for his films, which is more than any other person in history.

WOW!

31 MAY

One of the RAREST FISH in the world live in DEATH VALLEY, USA – one of the HARSHEST ENVIRONMENTS on Earth. The **DEVILS HOLE PUPFISH** only lives in the WATER-FILLED CAVERN of Devils Hole, where the 33°C water temperatures and LOW OXYGEN levels are LETHAL to most other fish.

1 JUNE

The **EIFFEL TOWER** was the **TALLEST STRUCTURE** in the world when it was completed in 1889. It stands **324 METRES** high and is still the tallest structure in **PARIS**. The tower was built as a temporary exhibit meant to be **TORN DOWN** after **20 YEARS**. Happily it survived and is now the world's most popular **TOURIST ATTRACTION**.

2 JUNE

TASMANIAN DEVIL

is not a type of demon but the world's largest meat-eating marsupial (mammals that carry their young in a pouch). It was named for its very loud night-time screech.

3 JUNE

CAVE PAINTINGS are

works of art drawn on the walls of caverns and rock faces by our ancestors. Often they show animals such as bison, horses and deer. The oldest cave paintings were created 64,000 years ago and are simple hand patterns.

4 JUNE

A **HURRICANE** is a storm with very strong winds that is shaped like a spinning spiral. Hurricanes form over warm tropical seas. They turn anti-clockwise in the northern hemisphere and clockwise in the southern hemisphere.

5 JUNE

CARTOGRAPHY is another word

for map-making. People have been creating maps for thousands of years. Ptolemy was a Greek mathematician who wrote an important book on maps in 150 CE. Today's cartographers use satellite images and GPS to create super-accurate maps.

6 JUNE

Millions of **ASTEROIDS** orbit the Sun in a belt between Mars and Jupiter. Some are the size of sand grains. Others are huge – Vesta is 525 kilometres in diameter. The asteroid Ida has its own tiny moon, called Dactyl.

7 JUNE

ELECTRIC EELS are not actually eels – but they are electric! They are a type of fish closely related to carp. They have special organs that can deliver powerful electric charges of up to 600 volts – enough to knock a horse off its feet.

8 JUNE

GIRAFFES have **DARK**, almost **BLACK**, **TONGUES! SCIENTISTS** think that this is so they don't get **SUNBURNT** while they **EAT**.

9 JUNE

LAMBERT GLACIER

in Antarctica is the biggest glacier in the world. It is 80 kilometres wide, 400 kilometres long and about 2,500 metres deep. It is also the world's fastest glacier, moving at 400–800 metres every year.

10 JUNE

There are more than 25,000 ISLANDS in the Pacific Ocean. Japan is made up of over 3,000 islands. Indonesia has more than 17,000 islands, making it the largest archipelago in the world!

11 JUNE

A HOVERCRAFT is a vehicle that floats on a cushion of air, which allows it to travel over land, sea or ice. The hovercraft's inventor, engineer Christopher Cockerell, got the idea when he was experimenting with a coffee can, a cat food can and a hairdryer!

12 JUNE

SUPERGLUE

Sticky situation

was discovered by accident. Dr Harry Coover was trying to make clear plastic gun sights during the Second World War when he created the very sticky substance. It was useless for aiming guns but amazing at making things stay put!

13 JUNE

The **BBC** was founded in 1922 and is the world's oldest national broadcaster. It's also the biggest broadcaster in the world – over 22,000 people work there.

Super structure

14 JUNE

The **LEANING TOWER OF PISA** is BANANA-SHAPED. The tower started to **LEAN** soon after construction started due to SOFT SOIL underneath the foundations. **BUILDERS** later tried to CORRECT the tilt, creating a **CURVE!** The tower has now been STABILISED but it is still 4.5 metres off-centre.

15 JUNE

BUDDHISM is 2,500 years old and is followed by 350 million Buddhists worldwide. Buddhism began in northeastern India and is the main religion in many Asian countries.

16 JUNE

The **GREENLAND SHARK** is the longest-living vertebrate (vertebrates are animals with a backbone, which includes fish, amphibians, reptiles, birds and mammals). They can live to be more than 500 years old.

17 JUNE

Scientists in New Mexico, USA, created a substance that is hotter than the core of the Sun. Their **'PLASMA'** or vaporised tungsten was heated by a magnetic field to 2 billion °Celsius – the Sun's core is only 150 million °Celsius.

18 JUNE

A **GYROSCOPE** is a spinning wheel set in a frame that seems to defy gravity! Gyroscopes can help with navigation and are used in ships, planes, spacecraft and robots.

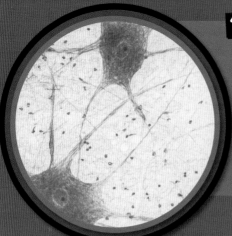

19 JUNE

You have around 60 kilometres of **NERVE CELLS** in your body! Nerve cells send billions of messages to your brain and between different parts of your body every single second. Nerves send information from your senses, which your brain processes to help you understand your surroundings.

20 JUNE

One of the WORLD'S LARGEST DELTAS forms on an inland sea. The OKAVANGO RIVER runs into the KALAHARI DESERT where in the wet season it can cover over 20,000 km², 95% of the water in the delta will EVAPORATE before it reaches the sea.

On this day...

21 JUNE

On this day, the **SUMMER SOLSTICE** usually falls. In the northern hemisphere the Sun reaches its highest point in the sky for the whole year and this day has the greatest amount of daylight. In the southern hemisphere this is the shortest day. This is reversed in the northern hemisphere on the winter solstice on 21 December.

22 JUNE

DIAMONDS are the hardest substance in the world, but they are made from carbon which also forms graphite – a very soft substance. Graphite is so soft that it is used to make pencil leads.

23 JUNE

George Nissen invented the **TRAMPOLINE** when he was only 16 years old. The keen young gymnast saw trapeze artists drop into a net after their act and thought it would be more fun if they bounced back up! His first trampoline had a metal frame with canvas stretched over it. George later perfected his design with bouncy springs.

24 JUNE

Tropical RAINFORESTS cover only about 6% of the Earth, but are home to over 50% of our animal species. Rainforests are important because they help regulate the Earth's temperature and they supply valuable fresh water to the atmosphere.

25 JUNE

CAMOUFLAGE helps animals hide from predators or sneak up on their prey. Jaguars' patterned fur blends into the sun-dappled forest floor. Three-toed sloths have green algae growing in their fur to help them hide among the trees. Coral crabs stick polyps to their shells so they look like part of a coral reef.

26 JUNE

Forget Willy Wonka! The real world's largest CHOCOLATE FACTORY is called Barry Callebaut's and it's in Wieze, Belgium. The factory makes 1,000 tonnes of chocolate every single day.

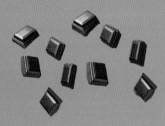

27 JUNE

VAMPIRE BATS suck blood from sleeping cows, pigs, horses, and birds. Very rarely will they bite humans for blood. Every night vampire bats drink about half their own body weight in blood. If they can't find a blood meal two nights in a row then they will starve to death.

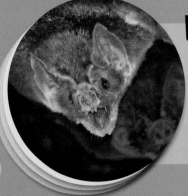

28 JUNE

A **SNOWFLAKE** is a single crystal of ice that has formed around a tiny speck of dust. There are 8 basic shapes of snowflakes, but there are so many possible combinations of crystal forms that no two snowflakes are identical. Snowflakes are normally small but single flakes almost 1.8 centimetres in diameter have been seen.

29 JUNE

Furry friends

SEA OTTERS hold hands when they sleep so they do not drift apart in the water. Unlike other sea dwelling animals, they don't have blubber but they do have thick fur that traps air to keep them warm.

30 JUNE

On this day...

TOWER BRIDGE in London is a bascule bridge. Its roadway is made of two bascules (or movable spans) that lift up to let ships pass through the bridge. Tower Bridge was first opened to traffic on this day in 1894. It is sometimes confused with London Bridge which is actually 800 metres upstream.

1 JULY

The **BOWHEAD WHALE** has the LARGEST MOUTH of any animal. It could SWALLOW A MINIBUS! But the whale actually only eats TINY SEA CREATURES.

⟨⟨⟨ Monster mouth

2 JULY

The **MALDIVES** is a group of 1,190 coral islands in the Indian Ocean. The islands have the lowest terrain of any country in the world – more than 80% of land is less than 1 metre above sea level. Unfortunately, if global warming continues as its current rate, the Maldives could be lost below the waves by 2050.

3 JULY

The **PRIME MERIDIAN** is an imaginary line of 0° longitude that runs through Greenwich in London. It divides the world into Eastern and Western hemispheres and is vital for map coordinates. The meridian is also where the world's time zones are measured from.

4 JULY

Time to be amazed – the **MAKKAH CLOCK ROYAL TOWER** in Mecca has the world's largest clock face with 4 faces measuring 43 metres in diameter. The tower itself is the world's 3rd tallest building at 601 metres high. There's no excuse for being late in Mecca!

5 JULY

PANGOLINS' scales are made from keratin which is the same material as your fingernails. They are the only mammals to be wholly covered in scales.

6 JULY

CATS first lived with humans over 9,500 years ago. Cats sleep around 12 – 16 hours a day to save energy. Your cat has a noseprint as unique as a fingerprint!

7 JULY

JUPITER is by far the biggest planet. Its mass is more than twice all the other planets added together. It is 142,984 kilometres in diameter – more than 11 planet Earths. Jupiter has 79 moons!

Out of this world

8 JULY

A **MANTIS SHRIMP** can punch with the force of a bullet. The shrimp builds power in its club-like front leg and then strikes its prey 50 times faster than the blink of an eye – the same speed as a .22 calibre bullet. The force is 100 times that of its weight, making it the strongest self-powered strike by any animal.

Packs a punch

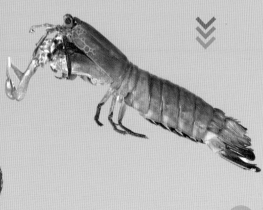

9 JULY

On this day in 1877 the first ever tennis championships at **WIMBLEDON** were served up. Wimbledon is the oldest of the four biggest tennis tournaments, called 'Grand Slam' events. It is also the only Grand Slam tournament that is still played on grass.

10 JULY

The **GREAT BARRIER REEF** in **AUSTRALIA** is the **WORLD'S LARGEST REEF.** It stretches for more than **2,300 KILOMETRES** – the distance from London to Gibraltar. It was built by **CORALS.** which are tiny **MARINE ANIMALS.**

11 JULY

HUMMINGBIRDS can fly upside down and backwards. There are hundreds of species of hummingbirds with the smallest weighing about the same as a paperclip.

12 JULY

The LARGE HADRON COLLIDER is the biggest machine in the world. This is a huge circular tube 27 kilometres long that lies deep underground beneath the France/Switzerland border. Scientists use it to smash tiny particles together. The results help them test theories about physics and matter itself.

Sweet treat

13 JULY

CANDY FLOSS was invented by a dentist. In 1897, William Morrison invented this fairground treat that is made of melted sugar spun into threads thinner than a human hair. It might be bad for your teeth, but it is very tasty!

14 JULY

The original **OLYMPIC GAMES** were first held in 776 BCE in Greece. They were held to honour the gods, particularly Zeus. Events included running, wrestling, discus, javelin and horse-riding. All athletes competed in the nude!

15 JULY

BATS use echolocation to fly and hunt in total darkness. They make sounds and then listen to the echoes to work out where objects are around them. They can tell how far away an object is, its size, shape and density, and which direction it is moving in. The sounds bats use to echolocate are too high for humans to hear.

16 JULY

ISLAM is the world's second-largest religion. It has around 1.9 billion followers, who are known as Muslim. Like Christians and Jews, Muslims believe in a single God, who they call Allah, the Arabic name for God.

17 JULY

Children don't have **KNEECAPS** until they are 3 years old. The kneecap bone, or patella, is made of a squishy substance called cartilage when we are born. When we are toddlers, the patella hardens into proper bone.

QUEEN ELIZABETH II was QUEEN OF BRITAIN for over **70 YEARS!** She RULED from 1952 to 2022, making her the LONGEST REIGNING female monarch in HISTORY.

How long?!

19 JULY

The **DEAD SEA** lies at 422 metres below sea level – the lowest point of land on Earth's surface. It is one of the world's saltiest lakes – since our body weight is lighter than the density of the water, you don't need to swim to float in it. The salty waters have been used as a health spa for over 2,000 years!

20 JULY

On this day in 1969, human beings stepped onto the **MOON** for the first time. Neil Armstrong made the first steps followed by Buzz Aldrin 19 minutes later. 12 people have walked on the Moon but there have been no human landings since 1972. This should change in 2024 when the Artemis mission returns humans to our closest space neighbour.

On this day...

21 JULY

MOHS SCALE

measures the hardness of a substance. This runs from talcum powder, which is very soft and measures 1 on the scale, to diamond which measures 10 and is the hardest known mineral.

22 JULY

Roy Sullivan was a park ranger who was **STRUCK BY LIGHTNING** on 7 different occasions. Roy also claims he had to defend himself from an attacking bear 22 times in his life. Talk about unlucky!

23 JULY

Cool country

CANADA has the LONGEST COAST of any COUNTRY with 243,042 kilometres of shoreline. More than half of all the LAKES in the world are in Canada – there are more than 3 million. The TRANS-CANADA HIGHWAY runs across the country for 7,821 kilometres – the LONGEST NATIONAL HIGHWAY in the world.

24 JULY

VANILLA is the number 1 flavour of ice cream. Real vanilla flavour comes from the dried seed pod of an orchid that is only found in Mexico. This orchid is very difficult to grow and real vanilla is the second-most expensive spice in the world after saffron.

25 JULY

The **CALIFORNIA GROUND SQUIRREL** chews up rattlesnake skin into a paste and smears it on its tail to confuse predatory rattlesnakes.

Sneaky squirrel

26 JULY

SIMONE BILES is one of the greatest gymnasts of all time. She has won 25 World Championship medals – more than any other gymnast – plus she has 7 Olympic medals. Simone has created new gymnastic feats – 4 gymnastic moves are named after her. She was the first female gymnast to successfully perform the Yurchenko double pike move in competition.

Sporting superstar

27 JULY

The **GULF OF CORRYVRECKAN** off the west coast of Scotland has one of the largest whirlpools in the world. As the rushing tide passes through a narrow strait the peculiar rocks on the seafloor create a huge swirling vortex. The waves of the whirlpool can reach 9 metres in height and its roar waters can be heard 16 kilometres away.

28 JULY

The longest and heaviest **FREIGHT TRAIN** ever had 682 cars and was 7.3 kilometres long. The train carried 82,000 tonnes of iron ore in Australia in 2001. The train needed 8 locomotives!

29 JULY

The **MUSCLES** in your **BODY** are made of **FIBRES** that contract to move you around. The **BIGGEST** muscle in your body is the gluteus maximus – your **BUTTOCKS!** You have **TINY** muscles that can move your **EYEBALL** five times a second to help you look around the world.

31 JULY

The **BLACK DEATH** was a fearsome plague that swept through Europe in the 14th century. It was spread by the bites of rats' fleas. It killed as many as 200 million people, in some countries up to half the population. Today we can treat this disease with antibiotics.

0 JULY

The **STONE AGE** is a period of time that began around 2.5 million years ago. Humans made stone tools and weapons, bone needles and flutes, and bows and arrows. Our ancestors learned how to farm and how to control fire – and first brought dogs into their homes!

1 AUGUST

KILLER WHALES are actually dolphins. Orcas, as they are usually known, are the largest member of the dolphin family. They are very intelligent animals and can live to be 90 years old.

2 AUGUST

The **TOWER OF LONDON** is a nearly 1,000-year-old fortress. It has housed a zoo, the Royal Mint and a prison. Many famous people were tortured and executed here. The Tower is also famous for its ravens, who are looked after by the Yeoman wardens, the Tower's guards. Ravens are the largest members of the crow family.

3 AUGUST

On this day...

On this day in 1492, **CHRISTOPHER COLUMBUS** set sail on his first voyage of discovery. He knew the Earth was round and wanted to find a way to reach Asia by going west. But he didn't realise how big our planet is and instead found a whole new continent across the Atlantic Ocean.

4 AUGUST

Nothing can travel faster than the SPEED OF LIGHT. Turn on your torch and the beam travels at an astonishing 300,000 kilometres per second. That means it could travel around the Earth 8 times in a single second.

5 AUGUST

RHINOCEROS horns are made from the same material as our hair and fingernails – KERATIN. The white rhino is the LARGEST of the 5 RHINOCEROS SPECIES and it can grow to 1.8 metres tall and WEIGH a massive 2,500 kilograms – the same as 30 MEN. A GROUP of rhinos is called a CRASH!

6 AUGUST

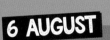

DOGS have a sense of smell that is at least 40 times better than ours. They also have amazing hearing and have 18 muscles that control their ears.

7 AUGUST

SATURN is famous for its rings – these aren't solid but are made up of billions of small chunks of ice and rock. The rings are over 270,000 kilometres across. Plus, if you could find a bath big enough to drop Saturn into, it would float. The planet has a rocky core but overall is 30% less dense than water!

8 AUGUST

SOUTH SUDAN is the youngest country in the world. It became independent from the Republic of Sudan in 2011. The capital city is Juba. South Sudan is landlocked, which means it is surrounded on all sides by other countries and has no access to the sea.

9 AUGUST

SHERLOCK HOLMES is the world's most famous fictional detective, created by writer Sir Arthur Conan Doyle. He was the original 'mastermind detective' with his magnifying glass and amazing powers of reasoning. Sherlock Holmes has appeared in more films and TV shows than any other fictional character.

10 AUGUST

The **ATLANTIC OCEAN** is the world's second-largest ocean. It covers 20% of the planet's surface. The Atlantic is home to the world's largest island – Greenland!

11 AUGUST

CHARLES LINDBERGH was the first person to fly solo non-stop over the Atlantic Ocean. In 1927 he flew 5,800 kilometres from New York to Paris in 33.5 hours. Today passenger planes make the journey in less than 7 hours.

12 AUGUST

The **MICROWAVE** oven was only invented thanks to a melted chocolate bar! In 1945 scientist Percy Spencer was experimenting with a magnetron, a part of a powerful radar system, when he noticed the chocolate in his pocket was hot and runny. This happy accident helped him build the first microwave and the very first thing that the sweet-toothed Percy cooked in it was popcorn!

13 AUGUST

GIRAFFES have the same number of **BONES** in their **NECK** as you do – **SEVEN!** They are the **TALLEST ANIMALS** on Earth and can reach 5.5 metres in height – taller than a **DOUBLE DECKER BUS**. They are **POWERFUL** too, and can **GALLOP** at 60 KM/H.

Cool creature

14 AUGUST

WHALES 'sing' to each other. These haunting sounds can travel 3,000 kilometres underwater. Whales use their songs to communicate with other members of their pod, or family, and to find a mate. Some scientists think they might also sing just for the fun of it!

15 AUGUST

JUDAISM is a religion that began nearly 4,000 years ago in the Middle East. Its followers are called Jews. The holy book of Judaism is called the Torah. Jews worship God in a building called a synagogue.

16 AUGUST

NINTENDO was founded in 1889. The **JAPANESE** video games company started out making **PLAYING CARDS** before moving into **ELECTRONICS** almost **100 YEARS LATER**.

17 AUGUST

BLOODLETTING was when doctors drained blood from patients to cure a disease. Bloodletting was based on an ancient medical system of the 4 'humors'. To stay healthy, your humors had to be in balance, which bloodletting was meant to help. But it was a painful and useless practice and it stopped in the 19th century.

18 AUGUST

You can tell how old a tree is by the number of **RINGS** in its trunk. Each year the tree grows a new ring. In 1964, a Bristlecone Pine tree was felled and found to be 5,000 years old.

19 AUGUST

GLASS is made from sand. This is mixed with lime and soda ash and then heated to extremely high temperatures. The mixture cools to form glass.

20 AUGUST

A TIDAL BORE is a constant wave caused by the incoming tide flowing up a funnel-shaped river mouth. The Qiantang River in China has a bore that can reach 9 metres high and travel at 40 km/h.

On this day...

21 AUGUST

The MONA LISA is such a valuable painting that it hangs behind bulletproof glass. It was painted by Leonardo da Vinci between 1503 and 1519 and shows a woman with a strange half-smile on her lips. The picture was stolen on this day in 1911 by a gallery worker who simply took it off the wall and hid it under his coat! It was found 2 years later.

22 AUGUST

LEONARDO DA VINCI

was more than an artist – he was also a musician, architect, anatomist, geologist, cartographer, botanist, writer, mathematician, engineer and inventor. He designed things far ahead of his time, including a calculator, a tank and a helicopter – over 420 years before the first helicopter actually flew.

23 AUGUST

Some countries have NICKNAMES. Thailand, in Asia, is known as the 'Land of Smiles'. Iceland, in Europe, is called the 'Land of Fire and Ice'. In South America, Chile has the nickname the 'Land of Poets'.

24 AUGUST

FOG is cloud that has formed at ground level – so you are walking through the clouds when the fog rolls in! Fog often forms at night when the air is coldest, and around bogs and rivers where the air is dampest. Fog is formed from millions of tiny water droplets hanging in the air.

25 AUGUST

Deep in a frozen hillside in the Arctic is a hidden vault, but it doesn't keep money safe – it stores seeds! The **SVALBARD GLOBAL SEED VAULT** is built in an abandoned coal mine and has concrete walls, sensors and airlocks to protect 1 million crop samples in case of a worldwide crisis. The seeds in the cool, dry vault will be safe for hundreds or even thousands of years.

26 AUGUST

There are around 60 species of **FLIGHTLESS BIRDS,** including the OSTRICH, EMU and RHEA. NEW ZEALAND has more species of flightless birds than any other country, including the KIWI, KAKAPO and WEKA. Until humans arrived in New Zealand 1,000 YEARS AGO, there were no large land PREDATORS in the country and flightless birds could FLOURISH.

Brilliant bird

27 AUGUST

WALES has MORE CASTLES per square kilometre than any other COUNTRY in the world. There are over 600 ANCIENT FORTIFICATIONS dotted around the landscape, including IRON AGE hill forts, ROMAN ruins, palaces of MEDIEVAL WELSH princes and bastions built by ENGLISH KINGS.

Cool castle

28 AUGUST

ELON MUSK is the richest person alive today, with a fortune of over £100 billion. But his riches are nothing compared to Mansa Musa, ruler of a huge West African empire in the 14th century. When he travelled to Mecca, Musa took 60,000 men and a train of camels carrying 18 tonnes of pure gold. He gave away so much gold in Cairo that he wrecked the local economy. Mansa Musa may have been worth the modern-day equivalent of £4 trillion!

29 AUGUST

THE GREAT FIRE OF LONDON

in 1666 destroyed 80% of the city's buildings. The fire started in a bakery. London's buildings were mostly wood and were crowded together so the fire spread easily. King Charles II ordered that the city be rebuilt in brick and stone to prevent a similar disaster.

30 AUGUST

The RENAISSANCE was a huge growth in art, creativity, science and culture from the 14th–17th centuries. The name comes from the French word for rebirth. The printing press was invented around 1440, allowing new ideas and learning to spread. Artists and thinkers of the Renaissance include Leonardo da Vinci, Michelangelo, William Shakespeare, Copernicus and Galileo.

31 AUGUST

Many fictional pirate captains, such as Long John Silver, Captain Hook and Jack Sparrow are based on a real man - BLACKBEARD. He was the most feared pirate on the seven seas. He had wild eyes and a huge beard, he drank rum with gunpowder in it and put burning fuses in his hair to look super-scary!

1 SEPTEMBER

If an **AXOLOTL LOSES A LEG** it simply **GROWS A NEW ONE!** Axolotls can **REGROW** almost any **BODY PART**, including the **TAIL**, **LIMBS** and bits of its **BRAIN!**

»»

2 SEPTEMBER

ALBERT EINSTEIN was a scientist who made many incredible discoveries. His Theory of Relativity helps us understand the movement of planets, the birth and death of stars, and strange objects such as black holes.

«««

3 SEPTEMBER

GIANT SEQUOIA

are the largest trees on Earth. They can grow up to 84 metres tall – almost as high as the Big Ben clock tower in London. They can be almost 9 metres in diameter and can live to be over 3,000 years old.

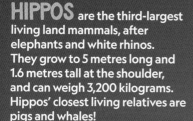

Terrific tree

4 SEPTEMBER

HIPPOS are the third-largest living land mammals, after elephants and white rhinos. They grow to 5 metres long and 1.6 metres tall at the shoulder, and can weigh 3,200 kilograms. Hippos' closest living relatives are pigs and whales!

5 SEPTEMBER

EASTER ISLAND is about as far away from land as it is possible to be – it lies 3,512 kilometres off the coast of Chile in the Pacific Ocean. The island is also known for its 887 moai. These huge statues were carved from solid lava by the island's inhabitants. Moai were carved to honour family members who died. The largest weighs 74 tonnes and is 9.8 metres tall.

85

6 SEPTEMBER

>>>

SATURN has at least 82 moons. Titan, the largest moon, is bigger than the planet Mercury. Titan is the only moon in the solar system to have an atmosphere. Methane, not water, rains down on the moon, creating dunes, rivers, lakes and seas.

Mega moon

7 SEPTEMBER

The **HIMALAYAS** are the world's largest and tallest mountain range. The range stretches for 2,500 kilometres across India, China, Nepal and Bhutan. The 15 highest mountains in the world are all in the Himalayas.

8 SEPTEMBER

DOLPHINS have names for each other. Each member of a pod, or group, has a unique whistle that is 'theirs'. Researchers confirmed this by recording the whistles. When the animals heard their own call played back to them, they responded!

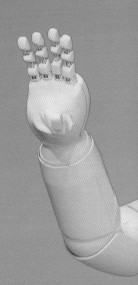

9 SEPTEMBER

PYTHONS are one of the largest snakes and some species can be 9 metres long. They are constrictors – they squeeze their prey to death and then swallow it whole. Bigger pythons can swallow mammals as big as monkeys, wallabies, antelope and pigs.

>>>

10 SEPTEMBER

EMOJI was recognised as the fastest growing language in the United Kingdom in 2015. The word emoji means 'picture' (e) + 'character' (moji) in Japanese.

11 SEPTEMBER

The INDIAN OCEAN is the warmest of the world's five oceans. The water temperature ranges from 19–30 °C – perfect for a dip!

12 SEPTEMBER

ASIMO is one of the world's most ADVANCED ROBOTS. This HUMANOID MACHINE can WALK on two legs, CLIMB stairs – and LEARN on its own! The WORD 'robot' comes from the CZECH word 'ROBOTA' which means 'forced labour'!

«

13 SEPTEMBER

The GREAT WALL OF CHINA is NOT VISIBLE from SPACE. However, there are lots of COOL FACTS about it that ARE TRUE. The wall is 21.196 KILOMETRES LONG making it the LONGEST STRUCTURE built by humans. It stands 15 METRES HIGH and 9 METRES WIDE and has around 25,000 WATCH TOWERS, shelters for soldiers and beacons to send SMOKE SIGNALS.

Super structure

14 SEPTEMBER

EVERGREEN TREES

don't need to cast off their leaves, or needles, because they are protected from the cold by a layer of waxy resin.

15 SEPTEMBER

STRATOLAUNCH is the aircraft with the biggest wingspan in history. Its wings measure 117 metres, which is longer than the pitch at Wembley stadium! The Stratolaunch is designed to carry rockets up to a height of 11,000 metres to save them blasting off from the ground.

16 SEPTEMBER

CHRISTIANITY is the most popular religion in the world. It has 2.3 billion followers. Christians follow the teachings of Jesus Christ, who lived in the Middle East 2,000 years ago.

17 SEPTEMBER

ICELAND'S glaciers are bigger than all the other glaciers in Europe put together. They cover 11% of the country's total area. Iceland also has around 30 active volcanoes as well as hot springs, geysers and mud pools. Iceland uses its natural geothermal energy to heat 85% of its homes.

89

18 SEPTEMBER

In 1858, there was a 'BIG STINK' in London when the hot summer made the sewage-filled Thames river unbearably smelly. The problem was solved by engineer Joseph Bazalgette who designed 1,800 kilometres of new sewers in the city. This mammoth project transformed the river and saved lives that would have been lost to disease.

19 SEPTEMBER

The GRAND CANYON is a SPECTACULAR GORGE that is 1.6 kilometres DEEP, 29 kilometres WIDE and 447 kilometres LONG. It was cut into the landscape over 5 MILLION YEARS by the COLORADO RIVER. There are over 1,000 CAVES in the walls of the canyon, but only around 300 have ever been explored.

20 SEPTEMBER

GALILEO was a famous mathematician and scientist, and was the first person to use a telescope to look at the night sky. In 1610 he became the first human to see the moons of Jupiter and the detail of craters on the Moon. He was imprisoned for saying – correctly – that the Earth revolves around the Sun.

21 SEPTEMBER

The word **'LASER'** is an acronym – its letters come from the words 'light amplification by stimulated emission of radiation'. Lasers work by pointing all the light rays in the same direction to make a focused beam. Astronauts used a laser to measure the distance between Earth and the Moon in 1969.

On this day...

22 SEPTEMBER

On this day in 1888 the first issue of the **NATIONAL GEOGRAPHIC MAGAZINE** was published! It is one of the most popular magazines of all time, with approximately 6.5 million copies sold every month. *National Geographic* features stories and photographs on science, geography, history, and world culture.

23 SEPTEMBER

The **THREE GORGES DAM** on the Yangtze River in China is the world's largest hydroelectric project. The dam is 2,335 metres long and 185 metres tall and it holds back such an immense weight of water that it slows the Earth's rotation, shortening the length of a day by 0.06 microseconds.

24 SEPTEMBER

A group of **PENGUINS** on land is called a waddle – on water it is called a raft! The Little Blue penguin is the world's smallest penguin at just 30 centimetres tall. In prehistoric times there was a penguin the size of humans!

25 SEPTEMBER

COWS have best friends and studies show they are calmer and smarter when spending time with their favourite friend. On the other hand, they can hold grudges too!

26 SEPTEMBER

The **ANCIENT BABYLONIANS** counted using a system based on the number 60. The number is useful because lots of other numbers divide evenly into it – 2, 3, 4, 5, 6, 10, 12 15, 20 and 30. Their system is still around today: there are 60 seconds in a minute, 60 minutes in an hour and 360 (60 × 6) degrees in a circle.

The **STAR-NOSED MOLE** has the **FASTEST REACTIONS** of any animal. The mole uses very **SENSITIVE TENDRILS** on its **SNOUT** to sense for food and in just 230 **MILLISECONDS** it can check that a grub or bug is edible and **GOBBLE** it up. That's twice as fast as a **HUMAN** driver can see a **RED TRAFFIC LIGHT** and hit the brakes (650 milliseconds).

Rapid reactions

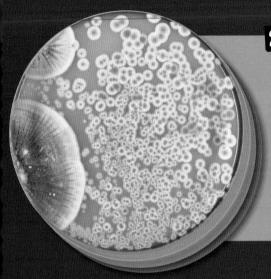

28 SEPTEMBER

On this day in 1928, Dr Alexander Fleming came back from holiday to his laboratory. He tidied his desk and in the mess found a dish with a strange growth in it – he had just discovered **PENICILLIN**, the world's first antibiotic and a medicine that would go on to save millions of lives.

29 SEPTEMBER

Some snakes, puffer fish and frogs produce deadly poisons, but the most toxic poison of all is made by a tiny bacteria. **BOTULINUM TOXIN** is so poisonous that just a gram could kill 1 million people. It is 7 million times more toxic than cobra venom.

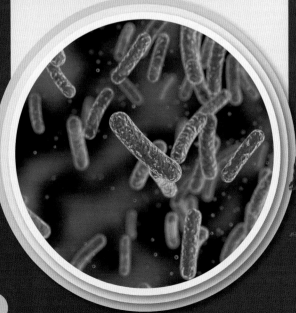

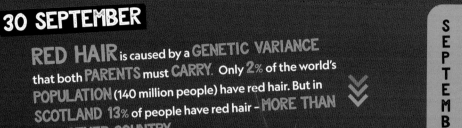

30 SEPTEMBER

RED HAIR is caused by a **GENETIC VARIANCE** that both **PARENTS** must **CARRY**. Only **2%** of the world's **POPULATION** (140 million people) have red hair. But in **SCOTLAND 13%** of people have red hair – **MORE THAN ANY OTHER COUNTRY**.

1 OCTOBER

SNOW LEOPARDS can't ROAR – instead they YOWL LOUDLY and make a **PUFFING** sound called a 'CHUFF'.

2 OCTOBER

The **UNICORN** is the national animal of Scotland. The unicorn may be mythical, but it was said to be a noble creature of great power and purity – perfect for a national symbol! You can see unicorns carved on many castles and other buildings in Scotland.

3 OCTOBER ⟫⟫

Leaves are green because of **CHLOROPHYLL**, which turns sunlight into energy for trees. There is less sunlight in winter and the icy cold would freeze the water in leaves, so in autumn deciduous trees suck the chlorophyll back. The leaves lose their green colour and fall from the tree. In spring, the tree turns over a new leaf!

4 OCTOBER

SKUNKS are black and white striped mammals that live in North America. When threatened they spray a foul-smelling liquid on their enemies. They can squirt this over 3 metres and it is such a disgusting odour that you can smell it almost 2 kilometres away!

Stinky squirter

5 OCTOBER

MACHU PICCHU is an abandoned stone city built by the Incas. It stands high on a mountain top in the jungle and is an amazing feat of construction. It was built around 1450 then later abandoned. It was rediscovered in 1911 by Hiram Bingham III, an American university professor.

6 OCTOBER

URANUS is the seventh planet from the Sun. All the other planets spin roughly upright, like a spinning top. But Uranus lies on its side and spins more like a rolling ball. Another planet-sized object collided with Uranus millions of years ago and knocked it over into this position!

>>>

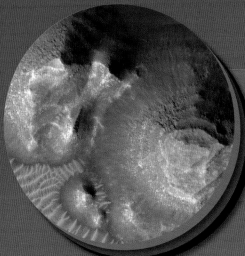

7 OCTOBER

OLYMPUS MONS is a volcano on Mars that is 2.5 times taller than Mount Everest. It rises 25 kilometres above the planet's surface and is the tallest mountain in our solar system.

8 OCTOBER

Can you imagine a waterfall 1,500 metres high with the water of 1,000 Amazon rivers pouring over it? Five million years ago the **MEDITERRANEAN** was a dry basin. Then the Atlantic Ocean poured through the Strait of Gibraltar to fill it, in a mega-waterfall called the Zanclean Flood.

9 OCTOBER

The **ARCTIC OCEAN** is the smallest and shallowest of the world's 5 oceans. It is also the coldest. Unfortunately its areas of sea ice are shrinking due to climate change.

10 OCTOBER

TOKYO is the world's TOP METROPOLIS, with over **37 MILLION PEOPLE LIVING** in the greater Tokyo area – more than any other city. That is 4 TIMES the population of **LONDON!** It is home to SHIBUYA CROSSING, the busiest pedestrian crossing on the PLANET.

11 OCTOBER

Mount Everest is the highest mountain above sea level at 8,848 metres. However the Earth is not a perfect sphere – it bulges slightly at the equator. **MOUNT CHIMBORAZO** in Ecuador is very close to the equator and its peak is the furthest point on Earth from Earth's centre. Its summit is 2,072 metres farther from Earth's centre than Mount Everest's summit.

12 OCTOBER

Mount Everest is not the tallest mountain on Earth. **MAUNA KEA,** a volcano on the Big Island of Hawaii, has its base deep under the Pacific Ocean. It rises more than 10,210 metres from base to peak, although its peak is 4,207 metres above the sea.

13 OCTOBER

CLEOPATRA, Queen of Egypt, lived nearer in time to the launch of Tesla cars than she did to the building of the pyramids. The pyramids were built around 2,500 BCE. Cleopatra died in 30 BCE, around 2,500 years later. But Tesla was founded in 2003, only 2,033 years after she lived.

14 OCTOBER

On this day...

Sound travels at 343 metres per second (1234 km/h) in air. It takes a lot of energy to fly faster than this speed and can be very dangerous. On this day in 1947 pilot **CHUCK YEAGER** became the first person in history to break the 'sound barrier' in his X-1 rocket-powered plane.

15 OCTOBER

FELIX BAUMGARTNER didn't need a vehicle to break the sound barrier. In 2012, this Austrian daredevil jumped from a balloon at a world-record height of 38,969.3 metre He then set the record for fastest-eve free-fall, reaching 1,357.64 km/h and punching through the sound barrier just a pressurised suit.

Smelly surprise

16 OCTOBER

SHOEBILLS live in the WETLANDS around the NILE RIVER in eastern AFRICA. They are easy to spot because of their LARGE BILL that looks like a WOODEN CLOG! Shoebills practice 'UROHYDROSIS' which means they POO on themselves to help COOL DOWN!

17 OCTOBER

The **COCO DE MER** is the world's largest and heaviest nut. The heart-shaped nut can grow to 50 centimetres in diameter and can weigh 25 kilograms. It grows on only two islands in the Seychelles archipelago in the Indian Ocean.

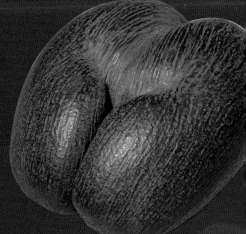

Medical marve

18 OCTOBER

Hot water can freeze faster than cold water. This strange occurrence is called the **MPEMBA EFFECT** after Erasto Mpemba, a Tanzanian schoolboy who wrote about it for a school essay when he was 13.

19 OCTOBER

The first successful human **HEART TRANSPLANT** was carried out in South Africa in 1967. The patient was 53-year-old Louis Washkansky, who received the heart of a 25-year-old woman, called Denise Darvall, who had been killed in a car accident. The surgeon was Dr Christiaan Barnard.

20 OCTOBER

NIAGRA FALLS are moving upstream! The falls formed 10,000 years ago and have eroded their way 11 kilometres upstream since then. They will reach Lake Erie and disappear in around 25,000 years.

21 OCTOBER

LAKE NATRON in TANZANIA can turn ANIMALS into STONE-LIKE CORPSES. The RED-COLOURED WATER of the lake is very ALKALINE, which is harmful to most animals. Birds and reptiles that fall into the lake often CANNOT ESCAPE and the salts in the water can PRESERVE their BODIES.

22 OCTOBER

Engineer Richard James was working on a device to help ships' instruments stay steady in rough seas when he knocked a metal coil off a shelf. The spring curved over itself and 'stepped' down to some books, then onto his desk, then the floor. Richard had just invented the **SLINKY** toy!

23 OCTOBER

A **SOLAR ECLIPSE** is when the MOON PASSES in front of the SUN and BLOCKS out its LIGHT to us on EARTH. The Moon fits almost exactly over the Sun, but is actually **400 TIMES SMALLER**. The Sun is 400 times further away, so this balances out exactly.

Out of this world!

24 OCTOBER

LAKE BAIKAL in Russia is the world's largest freshwater lake by volume. It is 640 kilometres long, 80 kilometres wide and up to 1,632 metres deep. It is also the world's oldest lake and was formed over 25 million years ago. The lake is fed by meltwater and is very clear – sometimes you can see 40 metres below the surface.

25 OCTOBER

HAILSTORMS form when rain is swept upwards by the air currents in a thunderstorm into freezing cold areas of the atmosphere. In extreme conditions, hailstones can be bigger than golf balls and can smash holes in house roofs. The largest hailstone ever was 22 centimetres across – the size of a large honeydew melon!

26 OCTOBER

Fantastic fossils

The oldest fossils ever found are **STROMATOLITES.** These were some of the earliest life forms on Earth, and they date back 3.5 billion years.

27 OCTOBER

The first cable under the Atlantic Ocean was laid in 1858 to carry telegraph messages. We can now communicate by radio and satellite, but there are still at least 37 working **TRANSATLANTIC CABLES.** The latest was laid by Google in 2021 and its 32 optical fibres can carry a total of 352 Terabits of data every second.

28 OCTOBER

MANDRILLS are the **LARGEST** of all **MONKEYS.** They are one of the most **COLOURFUL** of all mammals with their **BRIGHT** coloured **FACES** and **EYE-CATCHING** blue and red **BOTTOMS!** A group of mandrills is called a **TROOP.**

Cool colours

29 OCTOBER

A baby has over 300 **BONES** in its skeleton. Adults have 206 bones. As babies grow, some of their bones fuse together. Over half of all your bones are in your hands and your feet – the parts of your body that do the most detailed movements.

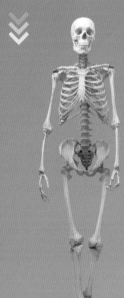

30 OCTOBER

ECHIDNAS are native to Australia. These prickly creatures are covered with spines and have no teeth. Echidnas are one of only two mammals that lay eggs – the other is the duck-billed platypus.

31 OCTOBER

Today is **HALLOWEEN**, the festival of all things scary and spooky. Halloween is based on the ancient Gaelic celebration of Samhain (pronounced SOW-in), which marked the end of harvest and the start of winter. On this day the spirits of the dead were said to return to earth...

On this day...

1 NOVEMBER

ELEPHANT SEALS look like blobs of blubber but they are extreme athletes. They can hold their breath for up to 2 hours and swim to a depth of more than 1,500 metres in search of food.

2 NOVEMBER

66 million years ago an **ASTEROID** 10 kilometres wide crashed into Earth by what is now the Yucatan peninsula in Mexico. This catastrophic event killed off the dinosaurs as well as 75% of all plant and animal species. The crater left by the impact is 120 kilometres across.

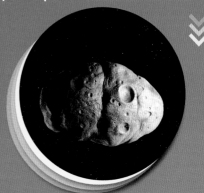

A need for speed

Massive migration

3 NOVEMBER

The **CHEETAH** is the fastest land animal with a top speed of nearly 130 km/h. But the peregrine falcon is the fastest creature – this bird of prey can stoop, or dive, at 390 km/h.

4 NOVEMBER

The **ARCTIC TERN** can fly over 30,000 kilometres per year. This bird migrates from the Arctic to the Antarctic and back again. This is the longest migration in the animal kingdom. It means the tern enjoys two summers every year!

5 NOVEMBER

LOSING at sport isn't fun, but at least you have never lost as badly as the football players of the team SO l'Emyrne in Madagascar. They were beaten 149–0 by rivals AS Adema in 2002!

6 NOVEMBER

The **COLOSSEUM** could fit over 50,000 SPECTATORS inside, where they would WATCH GLADIATORS FIGHT to the death as well as animal hunts and SPORTING EVENTS. The arena could also be FLOODED with water so that pretend NAVAL BATTLES could be staged for the CROWD!

Super structure

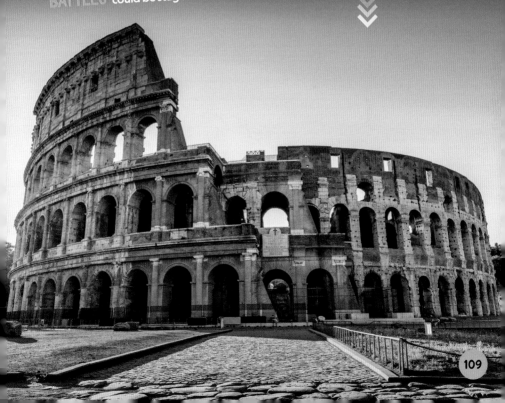

7 NOVEMBER

NEPTUNE is the outermost planet in the solar system, orbiting at 4,498 million kilometres from the Sun. That's 30 times further away than Earth. Neptune's year lasts for 165 Earth years.

Amazing artist

8 NOVEMBER

VINCENT VAN GOGH was a Dutch painter who painted like nobody else at the time. People did not like his art and he only sold one painting in his whole lifetime. After his death in 1890 his pictures became hugely popular. Today they sell for tens of millions of pounds.

9 NOVEMBER

The **CITY MONTESSORI SCHOOL** in Lucknow, India, is the biggest school in the world. It has 1,000 classrooms and 56,000 pupils.

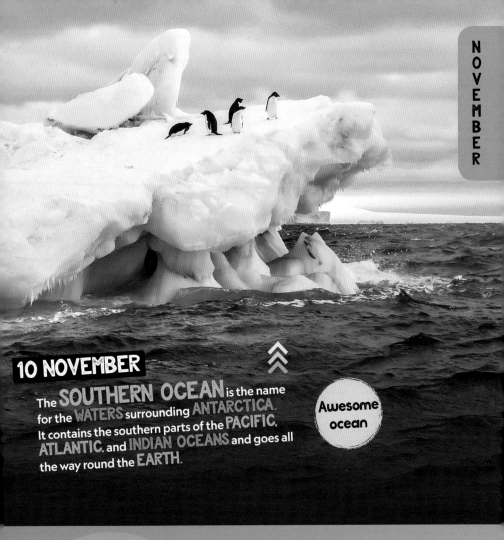

10 NOVEMBER

The SOUTHERN OCEAN is the name for the WATERS surrounding ANTARCTICA. It contains the southern parts of the PACIFIC, ATLANTIC, and INDIAN OCEANS and goes all the way round the EARTH.

Awesome ocean

11 NOVEMBER

The village of MAWSYNRAM in northern India is the wettest town in the world – 11.9 metres of rain falls here every year. That is 17 times the amount of rain that London gets!

12 NOVEMBER

The **ATACAMA DESERT** in SOUTH AMERICA is the **DRIEST PLACE** in the **WORLD**. Some parts of it have never experienced rain in their **RECORDED HISTORIES!** The **LANDSCAPE** is so dry and **ALIEN-LOOKING** that the Atacama has been used as a location for films set on **MARS**.

13 NOVEMBER

A **POLYGLOT** is a person who speaks many languages. Ziad Fazah, from Liberia, claims to be able to speak 59 languages. That's impressive, but Sir John Bowring, a Governor of Hong Kong in the 19th century, claimed to know 200 languages and be able to speak 100!

14 NOVEMBER

The **SILK** that spiders use to spin their webs with is stronger than steel of the same thickness. The silk is 1,000 times thinner than a human hair, and is made up of thousands of even thinner strands. Some silk can be stretched to 4 times its original length without breaking.

15 NOVEMBER

ANTEATERS don't have teeth, but their long tongues allow them to eat 35,000 ants and termites each day, which they swallow whole!

16 NOVEMBER

A **SUPERVOLCANO** is a volcano that has had an eruption at level 8 on the Volcanic Explosivity Index – the highest possible level. The supervolcanic crater at Yellowstone, USA, is 80 kilometres long by 45 kilometres wide – big enough to fit the world's largest city, Tokyo, inside.

17 NOVEMBER

CAMELS don't store water in their humps. Whether they have one hump or two, camels use them to store fat. This fat can give them the same amount of energy as three weeks' worth of food.

18 NOVEMBER

The **ROMAN EMPIRE** covered a huge area across Europe, North Africa and the Middle East. To make travelling easier the Romans built 400,000 kilometres of roads. Many of these were so well-constructed that you can still see them today.

19 NOVEMBER

HADRIAN'S WALL marked the NORTHWESTERN FRONTIER of the Roman Empire. This STONE RAMPART with a deep ditch ran for 117 kilometres right across northern ENGLAND. It took 15,000 MEN 6 years to build. The stone wall was 3 metres wide and 6 metres high.

20 NOVEMBER

JACQUES COUSTEAU

was a scientist and photographer who studied life in the world's oceans. He invented the Aqua-Lung underwater breathing apparatus and used it to make amazing films that showed people the wonders of the deep.

21 NOVEMBER

There are more CELLS in your body than there are stars in our galaxy. There are at least 100 billion stars in the Milky Way, but around 37 trillion cells in your body – 3,700 times as many!

22 NOVEMBER

CANALS were first built in ancient Mesopotamia around 2400 BCE. Today the Kiel canal, which connects the North Sea and the Baltic Sea, is the busiest in the world. It carries more ships than the Panama Canal and the Suez Canal combined.

23 NOVEMBER

FLYING FISH

don't actually fly by flapping their fins but they do leap up out of the water and use their fins to glide through the air. They can fly like this for up to 200 metres and travel at speeds of more than 70 km/h.

24 NOVEMBER

The GREAT LAKES are five lakes in North America: Superior, Huron, Michigan, Erie, and Ontario. More than 20% of all the world's freshwater is in the Great Lakes.

25 NOVEMBER

<<< **ELEPHANTS** spend up to **18 HOURS** every day **EATING GRASS, PLANTS** and FRUIT. They use their long **TRUNK** to **SNIFF** their food and lift it into their mouth. As well as eating a huge amount, the **WORLD'S LARGEST LAND ANIMAL** creates over 1 TONNE OF POO every week!

26 NOVEMBER

There are 1 million ANTS on Earth for every one human. Ants can lift 50 times their own weight – that would be like you picking up a hippopotamus! Ants are the only creatures besides humans that farm other animals. They shelter and care for aphids to get a constant supply of honeydew.

27 NOVEMBER

DNA stands for Deoxyribonucleic Acid. Every cell of every living thing contains DNA – it's like a blueprint for each organism. Information about the individual animal or plant – such as the colour of your eyes – is held in sections called genes. These are passed down from parents to children.

28 NOVEMBER

VITAMINS are nutrients that our bodies need to grow and be healthy. There are 13 different vitamins and our bodies make 2 of these – Vitamins D and K. We get the other vitamins by eating a healthy variety of foods, including lots of fruits and vegetables.

On this day...

29 NOVEMBER

Humans share around 99% of our DNA with **CHIMPANZEES,** making them our closest living relatives. We share a common ancestor that lived around 7 million years ago. Sometime after that our family trees diverged and we evolved into different species.

30 NOVEMBER

On this day in 1872 the first-ever **INTERNATIONAL FOOTBALL MATCH** was played. The two countries lining up at kick off were Scotland and England. The venue was a cricket ground in Glasgow with 4,000 spectators. The result? A boring 0–0 draw!

1 DECEMBER

The **MARMOT** is the largest member of the squirrel family. They can grow to be about the size of a beagle dog. Marmots live in the mountains, including the Alps in Europe and the Rocky Mountains in North America.

2 DECEMBER

ANGEL FALLS in Venezuela are the tallest waterfall in the world at 979 metres high. They were discovered in 1933 by a pilot called Jimmie Angel who flew over them. The falls are higher than the tallest mountain in England.

3 DECEMBER

The **COMPUTER** that helped the Apollo 11 spacecraft land on the Moon in 1969 had 4 kilobytes of memory. An ordinary mobile phone today has 4 gigabytes of memory – that is a million times more.

4 DECEMBER

AMBER looks like an orange gemstone, but really it is fossilised resin that seeped out of trees millions of years ago. Sometimes insects got stuck in the resin and these prehistoric bugs got preserved for us to see.

5 DECEMBER

The **GULF STREAM** is a warm ocean current that flows from west to east across the Atlantic. It carries over 100 million cubic metres of water per second, more than all the world's rivers combined. It's also the fastest ocean current, flowing at up to 9 km/h.

6 DECEMBER

DOLLY was a **SHEEP** born in **SCOTLAND** in 1996 who became **FAMOUS** around the world because she was the **FIRST MAMMAL** to be **CLONED**. Dolly showed that **ANIMAL CLONING** was possible and soon **SCIENTISTS** created clones of **PIGS**, **HORSES** and **COWS**.

7 DECEMBER

SILK is made by the silkworm, which is actually the caterpillar of a silk moth. These larvae love to feed on leaves of the white mulberry tree. Silkworms were first used by humans to make silk at least 5,000 years ago in China.

119

8 DECEMBER

PLUTO was called a planet when it was discovered in 1930. But there are many other objects of a similar size to it in the far reaches of the solar system. These cold little worlds are now called dwarf planets.

9 DECEMBER

SMARTPHONES are part of our everyday lives and in 2020 approximately 1.5 billion were sold around the world. But they didn't really exist before 2007. The Apple iPhone launched that year, putting a touchscreen mini-computer in millions of pockets.

10 DECEMBER

An **ARCHIPELAGO** is a group of islands. 'Archipelago' means 'chief sea' in Greek, but you can have an archipelago in a lake or river as well. The Malay Archipelago in Asia is the world's biggest and has over 25,000 islands.

11 DECEMBER

One third of the **NETHERLANDS** lies below sea level and the country's lowest point is 6.7 metres below sea level. The cold waters of the North Sea are kept back by an amazing system of dykes, dams, pumps and sand dunes.

Super speed

12 DECEMBER

USAIN 'LIGHTNING' BOLT is the **FASTEST SPRINTER** in **HISTORY**. He holds the **WORLD RECORD** at **100 METRES, 200 METRES** and the **4 X 100 METRES RELAY**. At the **OLYMPICS** he has won **8 GOLDS** and was the **FIRST PERSON** to win the men's 100-metre race 3 times.

13 DECEMBER

HERMIT CRABS ⟫

don't have their own SHELLS. They use the OLD SHELLS of other sea CREATURES. They particularly like WHELK shells. As they grow, they move out of their old shell and find a new, BIGGER one to CALL HOME!

Clever crab

14 DECEMBER

HIBERNATION is when

animals save energy by sleeping through the winter. Animals get ready for their winter sleep by eating extra food and storing it as fat. Bears hibernate if they live in a cold country, but species such as sun bears, which live in warm Southeast Asia, do not. Only three UK animals truly hibernate all the way through winter: hedgehogs, bats and dormice.

15 DECEMBER

The digital computer was invented 100 years before it was built. **CHARLES BABBAGE** designed his 'Analytical Engine' computer in 1837 but he did not have enough money to construct a model. The first working computer, called 'Z3', was completed in 1941.

16 DECEMBER

The **TALLEST HUMAN** in history was Robert Wadlow, who stood 2.72 metres (8 ft 11 in) tall. He was 1.83 metres (6 ft) tall at the age of 8. When he was 13 he stood 2.24 metres (7 ft 4 in) and was the world's tallest Boy Scout. As an adult he wore size 36 shoes.

18 DECEMBER

More **RED CRABS** live on Christmas Island than anywhere else in the world. Every year millions of them migrate at the same time, in a spectacular journey from the forest to the sea where they will breed.

17 DECEMBER

Eating **CARROTS** does not help you see in the dark. This is a myth that started during the Second World War. Carrots do have lots of Vitamin A and are definitely good for you, though!

19 DECEMBER

ORANGES are not naturally occurring fruits but in fact a hybrid of tangerines and pomelos.

20 DECEMBER

BLACK SAPOTE is a fruit that tastes like chocolate pudding. The fruit grows in Central and South America and when it's ripe has the flavour of rich chocolate and custard – delicious!

123

21 DECEMBER

In 1956, a **BOOK** was returned to the library of Sidney Sussex College, Cambridge – it was 287 years overdue! The book had been borrowed in 1668 by the father of the very first Prime Minister of Great Britain, Sir Robert Walpole. The book was called *Various historians of the Northern Germans and of neighbouring peoples*.

22 DECEMBER

Are you good at **KEEPIE-UPPIE?** In 2010 Dan Magness kept a football off the ground using just his feet, legs, shoulders and head for 26 hours! Beat that...

23 DECEMBER

EARMUFFS were invented by 15-year-old Chester Greenwood in 1873. His ears got cold when he was ice skating so he built a looped wire frame and asked his grandmother to sew beaver skins to it. He called his creation 'Greenwood's Champion Ear Protectors'.

24 DECEMBER

In traditional stories, SANTA CLAUS'S SLEIGH was pulled by **8 REINDEER.** Their names were: DASHER, DANCER, PRANCER, VIXEN, COMET, CUPID, DONNER and BLITZEN. Later on RUDOLPH with his red nose joined the flying reindeer crew, and Santa had 9 four-legged helpers!

25 DECEMBER

On this day...

On this day the birth of Jesus Christ is celebrated – it's CHRISTMAS DAY. But there is no mention in the Bible of Jesus being born on 25 December. He was probably born in spring. The date was chosen by Christians to fit in with the pagan festival of Saturnalia.

26 DECEMBER

ST PETER'S BASILICA in ROME, ITALY is the **LARGEST CHURCH** in the world. It is 220 METRES LONG, 150 METRES WIDE and its **DOME** is the tallest in the world at 136.6 metres. The dome was designed by the artist MICHELANGELO

27 DECEMBER

ST KILDA is a remote group of islands in the Atlantic Ocean 160 kilometres west of mainland Scotland. The islands were inhabited for over 2,000 years until they were abandoned overnight in 1930. The islands have the highest cliffs in the UK at 375 metres and are home to 1 million seabirds.

PRIME NUMBERS

2, 3, 5, 7, 11, 13, 17, 19, 23, 29, 31, 37, 41, 43, 47, 53, 59, 61, 67, 71, 73, 79, 83, 89, 97

Nifty numbers

28 DECEMBER

A **PRIME NUMBER** is a number that can only be divided by itself and 1. There are 25 prime numbers under 100, including 13, 47 and 89. The largest prime number yet found has 24,862,048 digits.

29 DECEMBER

CAPTAIN COOK was the first explorer to sail round New Zealand and he mapped thousands of miles of land. He was the first European to visit Hawaii, which was then ruled by ali'i nui (great king) Kalani'ōpu'u.

30 DECEMBER

The furthest a **PAPER PLANE** has flown is 77.134 metres. South Korean Kim Kyu Tae launched the plane in 2022 with the help of compatriot Shin Moo Joon (folder) and Malaysian Chee Yie Jian (designer).

HAPPY NEW YEAR

31 DECEMBER

At the end of this day, the first country to celebrate **NEW YEAR** will be Kiribati, an island nation in the Pacific Ocean. Kiribati's time is 14 hours ahead of London, in the earliest time zone on Earth. Celebrations are held in each village's 'maneaba' or meeting house.

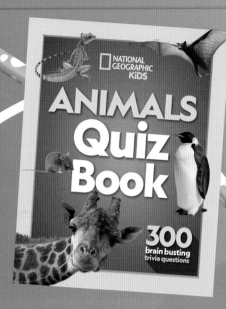

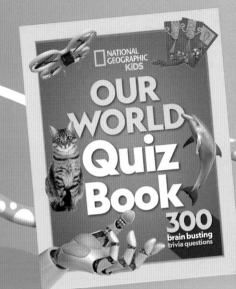

NATIONAL GEOGRAPHIC KiDS

Quiz books

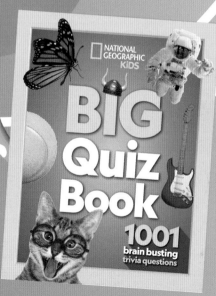